HOPE TO HEAR ...SOON

Janice Leasure Woodrum

Janice L. Woodrum

PREPARING THE WAY PUBLISHERS

PREPARING
THE WAY
PUBLISHERS

411 ZANDECKI ROAD
Chehalis, WA 98532 USA
WWW.PTWPublish.com

Janice Leasure Woodrum

HOPE TO HEAR SOON

ISBN 978- 0- 9821642- 7- 3

Printed in the United States of America

DEDICATION

This book is dedicated to all those who have sighed sighs or shed tears of desperation, needing to hear the voice of God in their hearts and lives.

As they read through the pages of this book, my prayer is that their hearts may be quickened to understand, receive and apply God's Word to them in new ways, to open fresh avenues of love and communication between themselves and God.

Isaiah once wrote:

"*The Sovereign Lord has given me an instructed tongue, to know the word that sustains the weary.*

He wakens me morning by morning, wakens my ear to listen like one being taught.

The Sovereign Lord has opened my ears, and I have not been rebellious. I have not drawn back."

Isaiah 50: 4-5

I pray for this anointing to be upon every heart and mind reading these words of the prophet Isaiah, that each new day will hold the quickening of a real and fresh hope to hear soon a word to sustain both ourselves and those around us who desire and need a touch from God. In Jesus' Name, Amen

Janice Woodrum

TABLE OF CONTENTS

Title Page	2
Copyright	3
Dedications	4
Table of Contents	5
Forward	8
Introduction	10
Chapter One – Honest	16
Chapter Two – Obedient	26
Chapter Three – Persuaded	34
Chapter Four – Expecting	42
Chapter Five – Trust	48
Chapter Six – Offering	54
Chapter Seven – Hunger	62
Chapter Eight – Empathy, Enjoyment, Encouragement	66
Chapter Nine – Abandonment	72
POEM: *Beautiful Encounters*	76
Chapter Ten – Resting	80
Chapter Eleven – Soon	90

TABLE OF CONTENTS

Chapter Twelve – Storms 94

POEM: *Pain and Promise* 95

POEM: *The Secret in the Storm* 115

Chapter Thirteen – Obstinate 120

Chapter Fourteen – Overconfidence 128

Chapter Fifteen – Need 134

SONG – *Hope to Hear Soon* 140

FOREWARD

Too many of us allow well-meaning Christians to put condemnation on us for one reason or another. When things aren't going right, often the first "loving" suggestion given is that there must be sin in our lives. And we "buy" it. The area of hearing from God is no exception. To be sure, if we have unconfessed sin, it must be dealt with, but in "*HOPE TO HEAR SOON,*" Janice Woodrum very refreshingly opens to us fourteen ways God may be wanting to effect growth in us. Only one of those has to do with possible disobedience or dealing with unconfessed sin. There are thirteen other lessons God may want to teach us.

To be sure, having open communication with our Lord and hearing from Him on a daily basis is absolute bliss. But, Janice does an excellent job of reminding us of the uniqueness of God and the varied methods He uses to conform us to His image. That may include a change in the way He chooses to speak (or not to speak) to us. She effectively supports her message with many Scriptures and illustrations.

Janice has earned the right to speak to us in this area because she is an intercessor. She has learned the value of hearing from God through the many hours spent in His presence. She has also experienced drought in her own life and thus has personally wrestled with this whole subject. I know Janice to be a woman of God, solid in her ability to hear His voice and obey it.

I was personally blessed and encouraged as I read the manuscript. I highly recommend "*HOPE TO HEAR SOON*" and pray that as you read it you may be set free from any condemnation Satan may have put on you. Furthermore, I pray that you may have your eyes and your heart opened to other ways God in His great love for you may be wanting to reveal Himself or "shore up" areas that need to be strengthened.

Joanne Krupp
Salem, Oregon

INTRODUCTION

"I sure hope to hear something from God soon!" Have these ever been your words? Of course, it's not the kind of exclamation we want to advertise. We usually don't even want to admit, except to our closest Christian brothers or sisters, that we have times when we're not hearing from God. Indeed, we sometimes don't even want to admit our condition to ourselves. But if we are really honest with ourselves, we will admit that we have had a season at some time in our Christian life when we were having a "dry spell," when we just didn't seem to sense the presence of the Lord as well as we had in the past, and we seemed to have trouble hearing His voice either in prayer or in our time in God's Word. We have heard this season referred to as a period of "darkness" or "drought," or even a "storm," and it is ever so uncomfortable for us, especially if we have come to a place in our Christian experience where sensing the presence of the Lord is especially valuable and meaningful to us, something to be sought above other life experiences. For most of us, this time of drought is not something we have necessarily tried to understand, but we have merely tried to get out of it as quickly as possible, for it makes us feel as if we have somehow failed – either failed God or failed ourselves, or both. We think we must have somehow fallen short, or this wouldn't be happening to us, because God never falls short.

I spoke to another Christian writer recently, who was editing a book he had written a few years ago. In this book he made a statement that the only reason for such a "drought" or "darkness" period was unconfessed sin. As I read this I couldn't quite agree with the statement, for I myself had already discovered another reason on my own, with the help of a very close Christian sister. So I began to pray about this particular phenomenon, because I think it is a common Christian experience, though we may not talk about it much or admit it to others. It bears research and discussion to attempt to understand it, because it can be terrifying or disheartening.

It can even lead us to despair if we don't know what is happening to us, or if we do not discern that the experience may be exactly what God has designed for our personal growth at the moment. If we have grown accustomed to experiencing a sense of God's presence, our first emotion when we don't sense Him near will often be fear, just as an eight-month-old baby begins to scream when mother goes out of the room. But as the baby soon matures and learns that mom is just in the next room, we can also learn that there are varied reasons why we might not keenly sense God's purposes in our lives in the midst of such a season. We don't need to be incapacitated with fear, if we understand this as part of God's discipline or training in our life of discipleship. The purpose of this study is to provide some illumination into the "dark" or "drought" seasons of our lives, so we can continue to walk steadfastly with God and grow in both our resolve and our ability to serve him faithfully as His disciples in all circumstances.

As I prayerfully examined some of the possible reasons for such seasons, I finally discovered that the acrostic "HOPE TO HEAR SOON" would help describe some of them. Perhaps as you consider these fourteen areas, you will discover some additional reasons of your own with the help of the Holy Spirit.

Chapter One

Honest

Have I been HONEST with God? John 4:23- 24 says that the Father seeks those who will worship Him in spirit and in truth. Have I brought my heartfelt worship motivated and led by the Holy Spirit who dwells in me, or have I relied on empty tradition or forms which have no real meaning? Have I been truthful with God about my real feelings, hurts, frustrations and desires; or have I pretended something else in His presence? God knows our hearts anyway. 1 Chron. 28:9 says "*...the Lord searches every heart and understands every motive behind the thoughts.*" He waits and longs for us to communicate in truth with Him so He can share truth with us. His silence might cause us to examine the real substance of our relationship with Him, and to be honest with both ourselves and God about the contents of our hearts.

A step to being honest with God is being honest first with ourselves. Sometimes we don't even know the things deep in our own heart which need the touch of God for healing, correction, or enlightenment. His Word is the sword which opens our hearts and reveals the truth hidden therein. Hebrews 4:12-13 says, *"For the Word of God is living and active. Sharper than any double-edged sword, it penetrates even to dividing soul and spirit, joints and marrow; it judges the thoughts and attitudes of the heart. Nothing in all creation is hidden from God's sight. Everything is uncovered and laid bare before the eyes of Him to whom we must give account."*

Sometimes if we are in a period of darkness or drought our tendency is to neglect our pattern of reading God's Word with some excuse such as, "I'm just not getting anything out of it," or "He just doesn't seem to be speaking to me." At times like this we need *even more* to persevere in the Word, trusting that our spirit can receive nourishment from God even when the intellect and emotions are convinced that there is no refreshment in the Word at such a season. The Word can pierce between soul and spirit, revealing the very thing which we need to know in order to be honest with ourselves and also with God.

I remember well a season in my life a number of years ago when I was just beginning to come into a period of revival after a number of years of "lukewarm" Christianity. I was a mother of children, but I was also working full time at a job I loved, and felt I was just beginning to come into the fullness of my career goals. It was a time when I was enjoying a new freshness in my times of praise and worship, and the Word was coming alive. And then I hit a snag because I wasn't being honest with myself or with God. I was starting to pray about many things in my life as my prayer life was restored to freshness. But one area which I did not dare pray about was my work experience. I did not want to subject this area to His scrutiny, because I was afraid of what He might say or what

He might require of me. He might ask me to slow down and work fewer hours; or even quit completely. I was not willing or ready to receive instruction from Him in this area, and therefore I withheld this entire part of my life from Him.

Then in His perfect timing, He chose to help me get past this stumbling block in my fresh walk with Him. I remember well that very black Friday. I had taken quite a fall in an athletic event a week earlier, and I saw a doctor that day about my swollen and painful knee. He informed me that I was going to need extensive surgery for repair of cartilage and ligaments which had been torn in the fall. Earlier that same day I had the unpleasant task of taking our beloved dog to the vet to be put to sleep for a disease beyond remedy. I would need to come home and break the news to the children.

When I got home I met my husband, who had also gone to the doctor for investigation of severe neck and shoulder pain he had been having. He informed me that he had a slipped disk in his neck, and would need immediate surgery. The weight of these three concurrent circumstances seemed almost unbearable. His neck problem was more urgent than my knee injury, so my surgery was postponed for later the next week. He would be going to surgery on Monday morning. On Sunday morning I came forward at the close of the church service for prayer from the elders, having just discovered the words in James 5:14, *"Is any one of you sick? He should call the elders of the Church to pray over him and anoint him with oil in the name of the Lord."* I was expecting physical healing, but God had something better in mind.

On Monday morning, my husband had already been taken to the hospital for his surgery, and I was meeting with the Lord in my very broken state. I was pouring my heart out to Him regarding my situation. I am usually very self-confident, composed, and in control of my situations. But because of the events which my loving Lord allowed, I was frightened, strung out, and feeling entirely out of control of these events which were swirling around me. In my weak state, He became strong, and broke through the hard core of my heart, that had tried so hard to hide from myself and from Him my fear of His investigation of the professional/career side of my life.

Suddenly, in the midst of my prayer time, I watched as the Holy Spirit did something I had not been able to do in my condition of strength and composure. Before I knew what was happening, He had pulled out of the closet of my heart this matter of my professional career and goals, and He put it on the altar before Father God. With a decision and strength which came entirely from the Holy Spirit, and not from my own strength, I found myself suddenly praying to fully surrender this part of my life to His scrutiny, trusting Him to advise me, change my heart, change me, or do whatever He wanted to do with it.

Immediately a sweet peace spread over me, and a sense of relief flooded in, because that corner of the closet of my heart had been emptied and given over to Him who has power to cleanse and heal. I realized that not only was my profession an idol before God, but another idol was exposed at the same time. That idol was my hobby of martial arts which seemed to take more time and effort as I pressed on to higher levels. I had justified this because it allowed me to spend more time with my children who were also studying Kung Fu. But it had become an idol, taking more and more time and dedication.

The Bible character, Jonah, discovered a wonderful truth about idols as he was within the belly of a whale, just beginning to turn his thoughts and prayers toward God in a way pleasing to Him. He prayed, "*Those who cling to worthless idols forfeit the grace that could be theirs*" (Jonah 2:8). Some idols in his life had prevented him from obeying God's command to take the message of repentance to the pagan and wicked city of Nineveh. In his near death experience he let go of these things, and began to cling to the living God, offering repentance and thanksgiving, while renewing his commitment to obey God.

Likewise, in the privacy of my own bedroom, I finally let go of my own idols of professional and recreational goals. A sweet grace flooded in and changed the direction of my life to one which led me away from professional notoriety and martial arts trophies. In the weeks and months following my knee surgery, I was separated from both my work and my practice of Kung Fu. In this time alone with God, He birthed a vision in my heart for a low income clinic for the poor – a vision that materialized over the next few years. And the path He had chosen for me led directly to ministry for Him in the years ahead. The Lord knew the real desire of my heart was to know Him better and serve in His Kingdom, rather than the world's.

In looking back, that bleak Friday was the turning point in my life leading to the life of ministry which I now delight in. The injury in my knee was so severe that most of the cartilage padding had to be removed, and for years I have had pain with long walks as bone grinds against bone. But when I experience pain, I rejoice with the words of David in Psalm 51:8, *"Let me hear joy and gladness; let the bones you have crushed rejoice."* The pain is a reminder of His love that was so great and wise as to stop me in my tracks, and open my heart to see the reality of the selfish thoughts and attitudes hidden there. He gave me grace to surrender these things to Him for His healing, correction and restructuring of my priorities in life.

In the dry or dark seasons of our lives, we need to continue to look for God's truth in His Word and seek Him in prayer, giving Him permission to search our hearts and reveal to us the things hidden there which might in part be limiting our communication, fellowship or full surrender to Him and His will for our lives. When we are honest with ourselves, we can begin to be honest with God. With this revelation comes the grace to let go of "worthless idols" and move on with God.

Chapter Two

Obedient

Have I been OBEDIENT?

Psalm 66:18-19 says, "*If I had cherished sin in my heart, the Lord would not have listened; but God has surely listened and heard my voice in prayer.*" Perhaps the most likely reason we are not hearing God's voice is that we have unconfessed sin in our lives. Confessing and repenting of the sin (turning away from it to walk in newness of life), can reopen lines of communication with God. We sin both by commission and by omission; in other words, we sin by doing things which displease God, and also by not doing things which He wants us to do. We usually tend to see the sins we have committed more clearly. But we need to ask ourselves if we have been disobedient by omission (i.e. neglecting to do that which God already told us to do). James 4:17 says, "*Anyone, then, who knows the good he ought to do and doesn't do it, sins.*" Jesus said in Matthew 25:23, "*You have been faithful with a few things; I will put you in charge of many things.*" God may not share new direction, revelation or instruction with us until we are faithful to obey that which He has already given us. If you are not hearing from God, perhaps you need to return to the altar where He last gave you instruction. If you have not followed through on His instructions to you, repent and ask forgiveness. Decide to and begin to obey His instruction and then wait upon God for further direction.

Let's go back to take a closer look at Jonah in the belly of the whale. He had been given a specific command from God to go to Nineveh to preach against their sins there, in hopes that they might repent and turn to God. Jonah was not pleased with this assignment, and he ran away from obeying God's directive. Through the terrible storm and loss of cargo, being tossed overboard and nearly drowning, and finally ending up a hostage in the belly of a whale, Jonah had not turned himself around to obey the Lord. And his life consisted of deep darkness, seeing and hearing nothing from God above the rumbling of the whale's belly. Amidst all of these circumstances, he did not hear another word from God until his attitude changed, he repented, and with a song of thanksgiving decided to turn and obey the word of direction which God had already given him.

We, like Jonah, may need to be confronted with difficult circumstances and a period of drought from experiencing God's presence until we examine ourselves and see if we, like Jonah, have avoided following His direction for our lives, or failed to do what He has specifically told us to do. Times like these should cause us to examine ourselves and pray, asking God to remind us of any specific directions He has already given which we have neglected to obey.

On the other hand, if we are in a dark or drought period in our life, but the Holy Spirit has not identified any area where we have not obeyed God's instruction to us, it is important that we keep doing what God has clearly revealed by His written or spoken Word before we came into this time. Psalm 119:11 says, "*I have hidden your Word in my heart that I might not sin against you.*" We need to continue in faithfulness, holding steadfast, trusting in those promises from God that we know. Galatians 6:9 says, "*Let us not become weary in doing good, for at the proper time we will reap a harvest if we do not give up.*"

Second Corinthians 5:7 says, "*We live by faith, not by sight.*" Even if we have a period when we don't keenly sense His presence or hear a fresh word from God, we need to continue to walk by faith in the truth we know, knowing that this too shall surely pass.

If a seventeen year old is instructed by his father to mow the lawn every week, he does not stop obeying this instruction, even if his dad is away for a six week trip. He knows his dad will return soon, and he wants to be found faithful in dad's eyes upon his return. A ten or 12-year-old may not follow through as well with this discipline. He will need experience in following directions faithfully, without needing constant reminders or nagging. Likewise, as we mature in our walk as disciples of Christ, we may need practice to learn to follow through with His instruction without constant reminders. A drought experience may be a part of God's training program for us as we increase in our faith, faithfulness and maturity as disciples of Christ.

After Christ's resurrection, and before His return to heaven, Jesus gave us very specific directions to "*go and make disciples of all nations, baptizing them in the name of the Father and of the Son and of the Holy Spirit, and teaching them to obey everything I have commanded you. And surely I am with you always, to the very end of the age*" (Matthew 28:19-20).

We all need to obey this command until He revokes it or gives us another one to take its place. All of us as His disciples are to work toward obeying this command in one way or another. We may be called to go across the street, the state, the nation, or around the world to make disciples. Or we may be called to help pay for others to go, or pray for others who go, or prepare others to go, or any combination of these. His promise "surely I am with you always" carries with it a very real awareness of His presence when we get involved in the Great Commission like this.

If you want more life in your fellowship with God, examine yourself to see if you are obeying His direction in this specific area of your life. This command is uttermost on God's heart, for *"God so loved the world that He gave His one and only Son that whoever believes in Him shall not perish but have eternal life"* (John 3:16). He gave the greatest price to win the world's lost; what are we doing to share the greatest burden on God's heart?

Chapter Three

Persuaded

Am I PERSUADED that God is with me, even when I don't feel His presence or hear His voice? Have I hidden the promises of God in my heart to sustain me in this time? Joshua 1:5, 9 says, "*As I was with Moses, so I will be with you; I will never leave you nor forsake you ... Have I not commanded you? Be strong and courageous. Do not be terrified; do not be discouraged, for the Lord your God will be with you wherever you go.*" In Matthew 28:20, God promises that He will be with us always, especially when we are about the work of making disciples for His kingdom. These are good verses to put to memory, keeping in mind that God's promises supersede our emotions.

We need to learn all we can of God's Word and His promises during the times when we have ample light of His presence, so we can fully trust in His presence in times of darkness. Are we fully persuaded of the truth of His presence?

As I consider the word "persuaded," I ask myself what makes a person persuaded. I thought of our system of trial by jury for a person suspected of committing a crime against society. If a trial jury makes a decision to charge a person guilty of a certain crime, they are fully persuaded, beyond any reasonable doubt that the person is guilty. If I examine the process further, I realize that it is the evidence presented by the prosecuting attorney which persuades them of the person's guilt. I wonder how we become fully persuaded that God is with us, even if we don't seem to be feeling His acute presence every moment, or if we are not hearing a fresh word from Him.

Romans 4:21 says that Abraham was *"fully persuaded that God had power to do what he had promised."* If we look at the story in Genesis chapter 18, we read about the word given to Abraham that Sarah would have a son at this time next year. The beginning of chapter 21 tells us about the birth of the promised son, Isaac. I have asked myself the question, "*How did Abraham become fully persuaded that God had power to do what he had promised?*" I came to the conclusion that there was concrete evidence that God had this power. What was the evidence? Chapter 19 tells us how his visitors had shared with him the plans to destroy Sodom and Gomorrah because of their wickedness. Abraham repeatedly questions the angels and they finally reply that if only ten righteous persons are found, the cities will not be destroyed. The angels went on, found less than ten righteous, and Lot and his family had to flee for their lives. The cities and the entire plain were destroyed by the burning sulfur. Lot's wife disobeyed the command not to look back and she turned to salt. These mighty acts of God were evidence that served to fully persuade Abraham that God had power to do what He had promised. The evidence which Abraham needed was in that experience.

If we look at Psalm 77, we see that the Psalmist is in anguish of heart because God doesn't seem to be hearing his prayers. He feels despondent, discouraged and too troubled to speak, wondering when he would hear from God. Then in verses 11-12, he discovers the evidence which sustains him: "*Then I thought, to this I will appeal: the years of the right hand of the Lord; yes, I will remember your miracles of long ago. I will meditate on all Your works and consider all Your mighty deeds.*" The Psalmist goes on to report about God's displays of power when He opened the Red Sea and rescued the people of Israel. He also recounts God's great power evidenced in the lightning, earthquakes and downpours of water. He remembers the evidence of God's great power in these circumstances, and remarks, "*Your path led through the sea, Your way through the mighty waters, though Your footprints were not seen.*" Though they could not see God, nor even experience His footprints, He led them by His mighty works. Likewise, we need to learn from this example, that when we don't seem to see or hear from God, or even see

His footprints ahead of us, we can take comfort in remembering His mighty deeds from the past. It is an excellent and necessary discipline for the disciple of Jesus Christ to keep a journal of some kind concerning his/her daily experience in the Word and in prayer, and a record of the way God has answered prayer and worked out the difficult situations of life. When we don't seem to be getting a current word from the Lord, we should read back through our journal and recount how faithful He has been in the past to hear and reply, though sometimes the answer we needed seemed slow in coming. Sometimes his word comes to us in a way that we do not expect.

In Habakkuk 2:1 the prophet says, *"I will stand at my watch and station myself on the ramparts; I will look to see what He will say to me, and what answer I am to give to this complaint."* And in verse 4 he says, "*Though it linger, wait for it; it will certainly come and will not delay.*" It seems strange that he doesn't say, "I *will listen to hear what he will say to me.*" Instead, he said, "I *will look to see what he will say to me...*"

When we don't seem to be hearing from God, we must ask ourselves if we are really looking for His mighty acts, both past and present. These may be the evidence that He has indeed spoken in the past, and the hope that He is going to speak now. But we must be encouraged by Habakkuk's reminder to wait for the word from God, even if it seems to be delayed. We can look for the evidence which will remind us and persuade us that God is present and active in our lives, even when we go through a temporary period of darkness or drought when His presence is not so clearly seen or heard.

We need opportunity to become fully persuaded in God's promise that He is present with us even when we are not acutely aware of His presence. This current season of relative silence from God may be a training ground for full persuasion. We need to keep a written record of these seasons, the events within them, our spiritual experiences within them, and what we finally discover God has been doing on our behalf during the period when we thought He was silent. He may be in process of developing just the evidence we need to be fully persuaded that He is present even during these periods when we don't hear or see Him so clearly. We must be teachable disciples, open to what He wants us to learn about following Him more closely even during these times. Psalms 32:8 in King James Version says, *"I will guide thee with mine eye."* Perhaps the Lord is trying to teach us a new kind of guidance which we have not yet learned. Lead on loving Lord.

Chapter Four

Expecting

Am I EXPECTING to hear from God, and preparing to receive the word He has for me? Isaiah 50:4-5 describes the expectancy with which Isaiah waited to hear from God morning by morning: "*The Sovereign Lord has given me an instructed tongue, to know the word that sustains the weary. He wakens me morning by morning, wakens my ear to listen like one being taught. The Sovereign Lord has opened my ears, and I have not been rebellious; I have not drawn back.*" Picture the days before sophisticated electronic equipment such as dictation systems and computers. The secretary waited with a pen and a tablet to write down the message or letter from her boss. Do we do likewise as we meet with our boss, our Lord Jesus Christ? When you come before Him in worship, prayer and study of His Word, have your pen and tablet ready to receive. He may want to share more than you can easily remember, and He wants you to record accurately what He tells you, so it can be shared accurately to "*sustain the weary.*"

Have you even been recounting an important experience to someone, only to discover half way through your story that your friend just wasn't listening? He was distracted, listening to something else, interrupting you to voice his own opinion, and oblivious to your desire to finish telling about an experience which you considered important. You soon got frustrated and quit telling your story, deciding to save it for someone who cares about you and who is really listening.

We have all had such an experience, and through it we should be able to identify a time when we have been such a listener. Unfortunately, we have often been like this when God had something important to say to us. We have been too busy with something else to take time to really listen for God's voice, or ponder long over His Word, waiting for a new revelation. Is it any wonder that He would cease to speak until we exhibit behavior which shows we are really listening? Do we need to repent of our disrespectful attitudes towards God and His Word, and turn the priorities of our lives around to give Him and His Word a greater place in our lives? Perhaps then we will notice a difference in our awareness of His presence.

My husband tells a story I love to recount. When he was a young man in the Lord, he would sometimes meet an old friend at various church functions or prayer meetings. This was an elderly man who had walked with God for many years. Every time the old saint would see Dave, he would ask, "What is God saying to you, Dave?" Dave would hum and haw and stumble to try to answer his question. But the truth was, Dave either had not been in the Word of God that day, or if he had read from his Bible, he had not been expecting God to really speak personally to him. He had been expecting perhaps only to learn some facts. Time after time the same situation presented itself, and time after time Dave would stumble for some answer – when in fact he could not really answer honestly that God had spoken to him, or what God had said. Finally, Dave got tired of this experience of humiliation before this godly elder saint. He decided that the next time he met with this saint, he would have and answer to give him. And so he began to read his Bible regularly, with a focus on an expectation that God would say something to him during that time and the prayer time accompanying it. Dave has been so very thankful for this one precious saint, who perhaps did more than any other teacher in his life to encourage him to meet with God daily in His Word and prayer, with an expectation that God would actually speak to him.

And because of this we have begun to make it a habit during our times in the Word and in prayer, to expect that God will have something specific to say to us each day. At the conclusion of each day's time with Him, I ask myself, "Now what did God say to me today?" This forces me to focus on what I read, and make a record in my journal of what I think

God is saying each day, with a list of questions about it for which I am still looking for answers. Begin to foster within yourselves and others the expectancy that God wants to and will speak to you regularly.

My husband likes to remind me of Exodus 3:14, where God tells Moses that His name is *"I AM,"* and also of several phrases in John chapters 6 and 8 where Jesus said, *"I am the bread of life" and "I am the light of the world."* God doesn't say "I was" or "I will be." He is *"I AM."* He wants us to remember that He is master of the present moment, ready to reveal Himself to us in the here and now of our circumstances.

Chapter Five

Trust

Have I continued to TRUST in God and His faithfulness, even in the season of darkness when I don't seem to hear Him speaking clearly or feel His presence? Faith is "*being sure of what we hope for and certain of what we do not see*" (Hebrews 11:1). Trust is a certainty based on your experience with God's faithfulness in the past. There is a subtle difference between the two.

I remember years ago to our first mission trip a number of years ago. We had never experienced receiving God's provision for airline tickets and other ministry expenses. We had to exercise our faith that God would provide for our needs as we sought to obey His word to us in fulfilling the Great

Commission. And indeed He did provide for our needs. When we made plans for our next mission trip, we began to look to God for our trip expenses, *trusting* that He would act on our behalf, providing for our tickets and ministry expenses. Trust is a certainty based on our past experiences with God's faithfulness.

We can enable ourselves to trust more fully in God by reminding ourselves in thanksgiving of His works on our behalf in the past, as the Psalmist did in Psalm 77.

Isaiah 50:10b says, *"Let him who walks in the dark, who has no light, trust in the name of the Lord and rely on his God."* And then he goes on in verse 11 to warn those who would want to resort to trusting in themselves, their own strength, wisdom or insight in a period of darkness. He warns that "you who light fires and provide yourselves with flaming torches ... you will lie down in torment." Second Peter 1: 3-4 says, "*His divine power has given us everything we need for life and godliness through our knowledge of Him who called us by his own glory and goodness. Through these He has given us*

His very great and precious promises, so that through them you may participate in the divine nature and escape the corruption in the world caused by evil desires." We must continue to trust in God's power and precious promises in times like these, walking in the light of His Word already given to us. We must resist the temptations to do things our own way in the flesh, (lighting fires and providing ourselves with flaming torches). We must encourage ourselves to hang on tightly to the words and promises He has already given us, sometimes needing to wait for some time before we get more insight or directions.

When we consider Genesis chapter 16, we are reminded of Abraham's promise from God in chapter 15 to give him a son from his own body. But Abraham went on to provide for himself the answer to his wife's infertility, and took her handmaid Hagar. The result of this effort has caused terrible torment, not only to Abraham and Sarah, but also to mankind to this very day, as the descendants of Ishmael and the descendants of Isaac continue to war with each other through the centuries, and will war until Jesus returns.

We need to take heed to Isaiah's words when we find ourselves in periods of darkness and relative silence, and *"trust in the name of the Lord and rely on his God"* (Isaiah 50:10b). Out of this trust springs the "hope to hear" again soon a new and fresh word from the presence of the Lord.

Chapter Six

Offering

Have I been bringing an OFFERING of thanksgiving and praise to God for His glorious presence and the wonder of hearing the voice of the almighty God, when I do hear and feel Him near? Humanly, we tend to draw near and share with those people who really seem to enjoy our fellowship, and likewise His heart longs to hear how much we love and appreciate our tender moments communing with Him. His Word says we are to "*enter His gates with thanksgiving and His courts with praise*" (Psalm 100:4). Are you bringing this kind of offering, or merely taking for granted the presence of God in your life? When we draw near to God's heart with our praise and worship, He is more likely to let us hear His heartbeat, as John did in John 13:25 when he laid his head on the chest of Christ in love and admiration.

After Job learned about the terrible disasters of losing family members, servants and possessions, Job said in chapter 1:20-21, *"Naked I came from my mother's womb, and naked I will depart. The Lord gave and the Lord has taken away; may the name of the Lord be praised."* Habakkuk 3:17-18 says *"Though the fig tree does not bud and there are no grapes on the vines; though the olive crop fails and the fields produce no food; though there are no sheep in the pen and no cattle in the stalls, yet I will rejoice in the Lord; I will be joyful in God my Savior."* In both of these passages, we see examples of giving praise to God within circumstances or severe loss, grief and lack.

First Thessalonians 5:16-18 says, *"Be joyful always; pray continually; give thanks in all circumstances, for this is God's will for you in Christ Jesus."* And Psalm 50:14-15, 23 say, *"Sacrifice thank offerings to God, fulfill your vows to the*

Most High, and call upon me in the day of trouble; I will deliver you, and you will honor me." Verse 23 says, *"He who sacrifices thank offerings honors me, and he prepares the way so that I may show him the salvation of God."* Perhaps God is testing our determination to give Him thanks in all circumstances. Will we pass the test, or give in to grumbling and complaining?

When I first became a mother, I read all I could about parenting, and learned that good behavior should be rewarded with positive reinforcement, and negative behavior should be rewarded with negative reinforcement. In other words, give praise and good things in response to the good behavior by the child, and a stern word or negative things (such as withholding a privilege) should follow bad behavior by the child.

For example, if my child asks me nicely for a treat, such as a sweet, I may reply "yes" or "no," depending on how soon the next meal is coming. If the child begins to stomp his feet and cry, or throws himself down on the floor, screaming for the treat, I will definitely NOT give him a treat at this time. I may, however, give him a word of discipline or a swat on the behind.

If on the other hand the child responds patiently, waiting for the appropriate time and speaking respectfully, and giving the appropriate "thank-you" when the snack is given, then I am eager to give the child the treat he wants. (This same process also works in training animals). God, the perfect parent, responds the same way. Grumbling, complaining and absence of the praise and worship due Him (because of who He is rather than for what He does), are behaviors which He will probably NOT reward with a sense of His near presence and a tender word of endearment or instruction. On the other hand, our praise and worship given to God even in difficult circumstances, and even when we do not seem to hear a specific word from Him for awhile, set the stage where God is free, able, and eager to reward us with deliverance from or through our trials, or a sense of His near presence and voice. Isaiah 30:18 says, "Yet the Lord longs to be gracious to you; He rises to show you compassion." I believe this same principle follows often in the Word and ways of God.

Psalm 50:14-15 gives us instruction in the following steps:

1) Sacrifice thank offerings to God.

(It is sometimes a real sacrifice when we don't feel thankful!)

2) Call on God in prayer.

3) God answers and delivers.

4) God is honored, and you give Him more praise and honor.

And verse 23 gives forth the principle that "Praise precedes deliverance." This principle is acted out numerous times in the Bible. For a good example, read 2 Chronicles chapter 20, where Jehoshaphat and his armies were facing an army far too powerful for them. God told them through the prophets to send the praise team out in front of the army, and when they did so, God fought the battle for them. Psalm 22:3 in the King James Version says that God inhabits the praises of His people. So positive behavior from God's people (including thanksgiving and praise, even in times of trial and loss) produces good things from God, including deliverance and an awareness of His divine presence.

Negative behavior (including grumbling and complaining) reaps negative things from God. Numbers

14:29-30 describes God's punishment for the grumbling, complaining and disbelief of his people: "In this desert your bodies will fall – every one of you twenty years old or more who was counted in the census and who has grumbled against me. Not one of you will enter the land I swore with uplifted hand to make your home, except Caleb son of Jephunneh and Joshua son of Nun."

Offerings of thanksgiving, praise, and worship to God are always appropriate. As we mature in our walk with God, we learn to receive both good and bad from His hand, learning more and more to trust *that "we know that in all things God works for the good of those who love him, who have been called according to his purpose"* (Romans 8:28). I believe He will sometimes allow us to experience dark or drought periods in order to help us learn these valuable lessons.

Chapter Seven

Hunger

Do I HUNGER for the presence of God and thirst for the sound of His voice and His living water? Psalm 42:1 says "*As the deer pants for streams of water, so my soul pants for God, for the living God.*" In the believer who is used to experiencing the presence of God, God will sometimes withdraw a sense of His presence and voice for two reasons. The first is to allow us to experience the sense of longing and hunger for Him alone. When we have fasted for many hours we experience a natural hunger which we can learn appreciate, even as we do the sensation of tasting the awaited meal. There is also a saying "absence can make the heart grow fonder." When we are separate from our loved ones for a season, it can intensify our appreciation, love and desire for them. When my husband and I are separated for several weeks for short term mission trips, we begin to long intensely for our fellowship together and our time together daily with God in prayer and His Word. When we are reunited there is a new appreciation for the opportunity to share our special fellowship with each other and with God. Likewise, there may be a silent or drought season in our lives, when God knows that this type of absence is the best way to stimulate our growth in fellowship with Him, and our appreciation for the opportunity to fellowship with Him as His children.

A second reason why God may withdraw our awareness of His presence (our awareness of His presence is a gift graciously given to us), is to provide an opportunity for us to see the true disposition of our hearts – are we hungry for His presence? In Song of Solomon 3:1-2 we read of the active pursuing of the beloved. In these times, are we inclined to pursue Him by every means we know, be it praise and worship, prayer, fasting, self-examination and confession, waiting upon God quietly, searching His Word, attending additional church or revival meetings, etc.? Hebrews 11:6 says that "*He rewards those who earnestly see Him.*" In a drought season like this will we slide into complacency, relying on form or religious tradition as a substitute, or will we seek Him with all our heart, soul, body and mind? Our hearts will reveal the answer, and God wants us to know the answer and to *"return again to our first love"* (Revelation 2:4).

Chapter Eight

Empathy

The E of "hear" stands for EMPATHY, ENJOYMENT, and ENCOURAGEMENT. As we begin to mature in our Christian lives, we appreciate more and more that "no man is an island," but that we are part of the body of Christ (1 Corinthians 12:14), knit together for many reasons, among them the three E's we will discuss now.

EMPATHY: 2 Corinthians 1:3 says that God "*comforts us in all our troubles, so that we can comfort those in any trouble with the comfort we ourselves have received from God.*" EMPATHY involves understanding, compassion and comfort. As we fellowship with or have opportunity to counsel other believers, these matters of feeling God's presence and hearing His voice are issues of grave concern for those who want to know God in more than a superficial way. As with all leadership training, God may first take us through such periods in order that we may be able not only to empathize with and comfort those in similar circumstances, but help them discern what God might be doing in their lives, and how to cooperate with his plans and Kingdom thinking.

Just knowing that there are other reasons for such a drought besides sin was a comfort to me, when a Christian sister shared the "hunger" teaching with me. Sometimes the enemy of our souls would like to convince us that sin is always the cause of such a season, or some kind of inadequacy in us, heaping condemnation on our already discouraged spirits. Sometimes satan's voice is very loud in these times, and we may be blown off course against the rocks of discouragement and our faith shipwrecked if we are not securely anchored in God and His Word (Hebrews 6:19). The enemy's first desire is to cause a separation between ourselves and God, and also between ourselves and other believers who can comfort us. A destructive sequence starts with separation and leads to isolation. Within isolation, discouragement and despair flourish; and then one is easy prey to the deception of the enemy. This deception of the enemy is almost always the same: "There is no hope for you in God."

When we ourselves pass through such a season, we can ask God for understanding which will help us guide and comfort others when they come into a similar time. If we look at Nehemiah 4:19-20, we see a valuable strategy used by the work force rebuilding the walls of Jerusalem. When one part of the wall would come under attack, they would sound a trumpet and the others would come around to assist them in the defense. This is a good lesson for us to follow. When we enter a drought season, we can pretend all is fine, not wanting in our pride or fear to admit our need. Or we can humble ourselves and blow the trumpet for the help of another.

Herein enters ENJOYMENT. God wants us to learn to truly enjoy and appreciate what He has given to others. So when we need a refreshing word from God we could "blow the trumpet" by saying to a partner in the faith, "I haven't heard anything fresh in the Spirit for a few days. What is God saying to you?" In essence, "May I have a drink of living water from your canteen? Mine is empty right now." This allows us to really ENJOY the word which the Lord has given to someone else, perhaps a new believer or someone just learning to feed on the Word and hear God's voice. As we enjoy and embrace the word that others have spoken into our lives, it can ENCOURAGE them to continue to seek God for "the word that sustains the weary" (Isaiah 50:4), while at the same time we are being encouraged ourselves. This pattern will cultivate in them expectancy for an opportunity to share an encouraging or healing word. In other words, they become progressively more eager to meet with God regularly with a real hope of sharing a word that they may receive from Him.

The expectancy that they can be used by God in the lives of others, may actually help such believers engage in the discipline and self-sacrifice necessary to consistently meet with God in a daily prayer and Bible study time. Have you ever considered that by asking a brother or sister for a "spiritual drink" you may actually be ENCOURAGING their discipleship in Christ, motivating them to fill their canteen regularly from the spring of living water found in Christ alone?

Chapter Nine

Abandonment

Is there an ABANDONMENT of ourselves to God's choices of how we will experience His presence? There are several reasons why God could let us experience a drought period in order to cause us to abandon ourselves to Him more fully.

The first can be stated: To help us give up our own notions that we must come into an awareness of His presence by certain methods such as through extensive or ecstatic worship times, in quietness alone, through a revelation from His Word, or by other familiar routines. Or we may think that we must experience His presence in a certain manner such as a solemn demeanor, laughter, joy, tears, trembling or shaking.

He may actually remove from us the awareness of His presence in ways we have grown accustomed to, in order for us to experience His presence in new and more inclusive ways.

In 1987, I experienced a revival in my Christian life and experience of God through the praise and worship tapes which had become popular. My luke-warm experience was transformed to a bright fire as I experienced afresh the delight of prolonged praise and worship. But I soon began to feel that this was the only way into God's presence. Of course, this needed to change, so He withdrew the opportunity to spend extended times in personal worship for a season. Soon I began to experience Him in new and fresh ways I hadn't discovered before, and the result was a much deeper "knowing" of him, and a more consistent "all day long" experience in a variety of manifestations of His presence. Then God was able to restore back to me the times of private praise and worship.

For instance, consider a couple who meet in the church and their only experience together is through the one or two hour worship service. They decide to get married and go to an elder for premarital counseling. He/she might give them wise counsel to get to know each other in a variety of other settings, such as long walks on the beach, dinners or gatherings with each other's extended families, studying the Bible and praying together apart from the Sunday worship service. Or they might enjoy discovering each other's favorite song, amusement park, food, TV show, music or books. The result would be a much broader knowing and appreciation of each other as they come together in different ways.

Likewise, God wants us to experience His presence in an endless variety of situations or methods – the absolute silence of a 2:00 a.m. wakeful period, the glory of a spectacular sunset or mountain view, His touch in a time of loss or grief or His voice of gentle correction through a loving friend. When we become willing to abandon ourselves to His many and varied choices of how He will manifest His presence, we are free to experience the surprise and delight of His presence where we many not have expected it before.

Secondly, God may remove the manner of expression of His presence in order to expand, broaden and deepen our experience of Him. We recently heard a report from a missionary teaching a leadership seminar in the Philippines. A number of different denominations were gathered together, some of them conservative in their manner of experiencing the presence of God. Some were completely transformed when during an altar time they suddenly found themselves melting to the floor by the overwhelming presence of the Holy Spirit, and enjoying the warmth of His presence as if stretched out on the beach basking in the sunshine.

The result was not only the broadening of their own experience of God's presence, but a new sense of understanding and unity with their brothers and sisters whom they had previously thought to be a little odd or extreme in their manner of experiencing God. When we are holding back, expecting only certain predictable or controllable manners of experience God's presence in our lives, He may withdraw these so we can experience a panorama of new and refreshing revelations of His presence. "Sorry, no vanilla today. Would you like to try mountain blackberry with a dash of pistachio?"

Consider the surprise of the disciples as they saw Jesus walking to them on the water during a storm (Matthew 14:22-31). Peter was first to embrace the new experience by walking to the Lord on the water. Yet, later in his walk with Lord, he did not cling to or demand this experience when he jumped from the boat and swam to the Lord on the shore in John 21:7.

Thirdly, it is possible that the method or manner of experiencing God may become the focus of our affection rather than God Himself. When the things of God begin to take precedence over the God of all things, He may remove the things we are seeking until He Himself is our focus. He is eternal; the experiences are transient and changing. We must not cling to the experiences of God, but cling to the God of our experiences – allowing our experiences to be varied, changing, mild or intense, traditional or contemporary. One of the most clear and significant evidences of the presence of

God is uniqueness ... such as every snowflake, every leaf, every flower, every grain of sand and every language.

Beautiful Encounter

By Amber Woodrum

I say, "Beautiful Encounter"...
At this world you've made.
"Beautiful Encounter"...
At the grass field, every blade.

I say, "Beautiful Encounter"...
At every color on every rose.
"Beautiful Encounter"...
At every sunset sky and the majesty it shows.

I say, "Beautiful Encounter"...
At every moonlit night.
"Beautiful Encounter"...
At the dawn's new light.

I say, "Beautiful Encounter"...
At every wave on every sea.
You say, "Beautiful Encounter"...
At every glimpse of me.

Chapter Ten

Resting

Am I RESTING in His sovereignty?

When we find that we are in a period of relative darkness or drought, we can learn to relax in the knowledge that He is in control of our experience, even though we are not. The enemy would like to convince us in these times that there is no hope, or that God has abandoned us. Psalm 130 gives us a good model for continuing to hope in God through these times. Verse 1 reads, "*Out of the depths I cry to you, O Lord; O Lord hear my voice. Let your ears be attentive to my cry for mercy.*" We are not sure what "the depths" are to the Psalmist, but it could be a period similar to what we have been discussing. In verses 3-5a he reminds himself of God's great mercy and forgiveness, which is good reason to fear the Lord: *"If you, O Lord, kept a record of sins, O Lord, who could stand? But with you there is forgiveness; therefore you are feared. I wait for the Lord..."*

If we find ourselves in a place of relative drought, it is of utmost importance that we do likewise. That is, to ask the Holy Spirit to search our hearts, revealing to us any unconfessed sin which might be causing God to turn His face from us. Isaiah 59:2 says, *"But your iniquities have separated you from your God; your sins have hidden His face from you, so that He will not hear."* In Psalm 130:5 the Psalmist then begins to wait, declaring his hope in God. Verses 5-6 read, *"I wait for the Lord, my soul waits, and in His Word I put my hope. My soul waits for the Lord more than watchmen wait for the morning, more than watchmen wait for the morning."* In verses 7-8 he encourages Israel to put their hope in the Lord, reminding them of His unfailing love and forgiveness of sins. *"O Israel, put your hope in the Lord, for with the Lord is unfailing love. He Himself will redeem Israel from all their sins."*

Hebrews 6:13-20 discusses the hope which Abraham held on to, trusting that he would receive what he hoped for in due season according to the promises of God. We are likewise encouraged in verses 19-20: *"We have this hope as an anchor for the soul, firm and secure. It enters the inner sanctuary behind the curtain, where Jesus, who went before us, has entered on our behalf. He has become a high priest forever, in the order of Melchizedek."* We are invited to put our anchor down at the very throne of God, where Jesus is constantly interceding for us according to Romans 8:34: *"Christ Jesus, who died – more than that, who was raised to life – is at the right hand of God and is also interceding for us."* We can rest in the work which He has done for us and continues to do, even in the periods of darkness, drought or storm.

I have been in a small boat on the Puget Sound near Seattle, Washington when darkness of night or a storm approached. This can be a very frightening experience, and sometimes there is nothing one can do except get as close to shore as possible and put down anchor until the night or storm is passed. With the anchor secure, we can rest during these times, knowing that neither the darkness nor storm will last forever. Verses 5 and 6 of Psalm 130, describe this kind of waiting experience. Lamentations 3:19-26 is a similar passage, where the writer reminds himself of God's great love and forgiveness, with mercies which are new every morning. Verse 24 says, *"I say to myself, 'The Lord is my portion; therefore I will wait for Him.' The Lord is good to those whose hope is in Him, to the one who seeks Him; it is good to wait quietly for the salvation of the Lord."*

Paul writes his letter to the Philippians from prison, with no immediate opportunity to visit and encourage his disciples there. In chapter 2:12-13 he writes, *"Therefore, my dear friends, as you have always obeyed – not only in my presence, but now much more in my absence – continue to work out your salvation with fear and trembling, for it is God who works in you to will and to act according to His good purpose."* He is encouraging them to continue in what he has taught them, even though he cannot be with them presently, and we find that Jesus taught similar progressive lessons of faith to his disciples while He was with them.

In Luke 8:22-25, we have the story of Jesus asleep in the boat when a squall came down on the lake, causing the disciples to fear for their lives. He quieted the storm and said to them, "Where is your faith?" At this point they didn't feel entirely safe even in His presence. In Mark 6:45-52 He gives them a lesson to stretch their faith a little farther. Verse 45 says, "*Jesus made His disciples get into the boat*" and go on ahead, while he went up on a mountainside to pray. A storm came upon them in the evening, and continued through the night, but Jesus was watching and praying for them. The Greek word for "made" (above) means *compelled*. Jesus had actually set up this situation for them to experience, in order to increase their faith when they couldn't see Him because of separation, darkness and storm. He finally came to them in the fourth watch of the night (between 3-6 a.m.) and calmed the storm. In Matthew's version of this story in chapter 14 we have the account of Peter's experience of walking on the water, and verse 32 tells us that the Holy Spirit used this experience to give greater revelation of who Jesus was: *"And when they climbed into the boat, the wind died down. Then those who were in the boat worshipped him, saying, 'Truly you are the Son of God.'"*

A much greater lesson came when Jesus died on the cross and was buried. We are all familiar with the sorrow and despair that the disciples experienced during the "grave" time, as recorded in the gospels. This separation almost left them without any hope. But following His resurrection, on the road to Emmaus (Luke 24:13-35) Jesus was gracious to gently explain and instruct them more clearly and completely about what the scriptures had predicted concerning the things which he had to suffer. Then they had forty days to walk and talk with Him again, learning even more about the Kingdom of God.

Finally, in Acts 1:11 we see the final chapter of these growing experiences in faith and trust: *"Men of Galilee" they said, "why do you stand here looking into the sky? This same Jesus, who has been taken from you into heaven, will come back in the same way you have seen him go into heaven."*

We, like the disciples, are a part of this same period, waiting for the return of Jesus, and like them we have been given the Holy Spirit to strengthen and encourage us during this time, reminding us and instructing us of all Jesus said and taught (John 14:26).

We could consider an eight-month-old baby, who begins to scream the moment mommy walks out of the room. Soon, as he becomes a little more mature, the baby learns that she is only in the next room, and he can play quietly in his crib or playpen for a short time, even though he can't see her for these minutes. Later he will learn to go to school, being comfortable without Mom for the length of a school day, and one day he will move out to go to college or marry. But he is still convinced of mother's love and concern for him, even though there may be periods of absence for months or years at a time.

These examples speak of a natural progression of faith and trust through increasing periods of separation from those we depend upon. Should it surprise us that Jesus might also allow us seasons when we do not see Him or hear His voice clearly, in order to increase our faith and trust in Him? If we read the gospels and Revelation, we are warned that in the end times there will be seasons of severe trial and persecution, and we may require some special training to "stand firm" with Him during these times. Let us consider how we can *rest* in His sovereignty during these times of instruction, putting down our anchor securely in Jesus and His promises, trusting that He knows best for us.

In Matthew 11:28-30, Jesus has clearly extended an invitation to us to enter into His rest; not a rest from work, but a rest within our work: "*Come to me, all you who are weary and burdened, and I will give you rest. Take my yoke upon you and learn from me, for I am gentle and humble in heart, and you will find rest for your souls. For my yoke is easy and my burden is light.*" The yoke is an instrument of work, and Jesus invites us to participate and cooperate with the work of the Holy Spirit in our lives. A portion of His work may be accomplished in our lives during relative periods of darkness, and we must *"make every effort to enter that rest..."* (Hebrews 4:11), trusting that in even this God is working sovereignly for our good. He wants us to continue to do in His absence what He last commanded us to do in His presence, that is to *"preach the gospel to all nations..."* (Matthew 28:20).

Chapter Eleven

Soon

It is finished with the word, "soon."

When I originally wrote this small book, I thought it was finished with the end of the word "hear," but I discovered there was more to examine in regard to the waiting to once again hear and feel the presence of God. It is the word "soon." When we are experiencing a drought, we pray for rain every day, and keep a close watch on the clouds for a sign that the climate may be changing. So it is in a spiritual drought period – we just want it to end. We want again that experience and refreshing of hearing God's voice clearly, and feeling His very near presence in the moments of our lives – like a gentle refreshing rain. A popular song has a line which says, "*Jesus,*

Jesus, Jesus ... like a fragrance after the rain." We want that cool, clean refreshing which comes in a gentle rain after the clouds of choking dust and grime. We want it sooner ... not later. Let's examine "soon", and see if there is yet another dimension in understanding these uncomfortable periods of our lives.

Chapter Twelve

Storm

Have you ever been in a thunder storm when the clapping of thunder, the pounding of rain and the rushing wind are so loud you have to yell at your companion in order to be heard? We have storms of life like this, when the current circumstances are so overwhelmingly torrential that we have trouble hearing the voice of God. They are times when we want to scream at God and shake our fist, "Why God?" ... "Why did my husband leave me and the children for another woman?" ... "Why did I get this terrible disease?" I wonder if Joni Eareckson Tada ever asked God, "Why did I have to break my neck?" In your mind you may be forming the words of your own question right now as you read these others. I know I have asked one of these questions, and the storm wasn't over in a day, or a week or even a year ... but it did pass. When we're caught out in a torrential rain, we could visualize at least two choices. We could stand outside getting thoroughly drenched, chilled and eventually sick, shaking our fist at God, yelling "Why, why...why?"

Pain and Promise

By Amber Woodrum

You look to the sky and wonder,
"How long will it rain?"
You're deaf from the thunder,
And drowning in its pain.
You question each cloud,
And long for blue skies...
Seems you'll never understand
Life's all-too-soon good-byes.
But, the promise for you is,
The weather will change.
There's hope in that promise,
As you look toward better days.
So, even though it seems
You've stood in the cold for too long;
And shivered through too many
Of the winds' sad songs...
There is One who has heard
Your whisper of a cry;
He sings over you now
With His healing lullaby.
And though today it may seem
That you struggle to hear...

His Songs of Deliverance will one day be clear.

We could stand out in the rain yelling at God, but the yelling doesn't usually bring comfort. Another option is to take cover in a hiding place. Corrie Ten Boom describes such a hiding place which she provided for persecuted Jews during World War II, and which she later found for herself in the cleft of the Rock, Jesus Christ in the midst of her suffering in a concentration camp. Both Joni and Corrie have written about the presence of God which they found in storms far more devastating than most of us have to face, and there are scores of other testimonies of those who have weathered the storms of circumstances and come out on the other side understanding at least some of the "why" of it.

A good friend called us last year to tell us his beautiful farm house had burned to the ground. Thankfully his wife and six children were not in the house when it burned. Since that time, he has discovered the "why" of it, and has a powerful testimony of how God has worked to make some dramatic life changes as a result. But sometimes it takes seasons and even years to understand these sorts of things. Isaiah 55:9 says,

"As the heavens are higher than the earth, so are my ways higher than your ways and my thoughts than your thoughts."

I think of a picture of a bouncy two year old, who is used to running into mom and dad's bed with a tale to tell, or just wanting a romp and a hug. But there are times when the bedroom door is shut and the two year old is not welcome in their bed. They may explain that mom and dad need time alone, but it will be many years before they explain to this child the details of sexual intimacy between a man and his wife.

Sometimes I think it's like that with the explanations God has for us regarding the events of our lives. Sometimes a full explanation of the "why" will just have to wait for God's selected timing for a greater revelation; after all He is the Father and the sovereign one. We are the children ... growing, maturing, and learning every day more about God's ways, His Word, and His Kingdom economy. Unfortunately we don't always see the "why" until the storm is long over, and sometimes even never.

So where is the comfort in the time of storm? When we shake our fist as the rain or snow or hail drenches us, yelling at God, we will seldom be able to hear His voice above our own. You might want to turn to I Kings chapter19 and review Elijah's struggle to hear God; and of all things it came after a great spiritual victory. We find God's voice was not in the wind, nor the earthquake, nor the fire ... but in a gentle whisper. And after he finished shaking his fist at God with his limited understanding, saying, "I am the only one left," God gently gave him more useful work to do for Him, explaining in the end, "I reserve seven thousand in Israel – all whose knees have not bowed down to Baal ..." God's view and perspective was much larger than his. He could only see himself as one, and God had thousands in His field of vision. In Joni and Corrie's cases, God had millions in His field of vision.

Where can we go to find that cleft in the rock, to weather the storm in the safety and security which only He can provide? The answer lies in God's faithfulness to His Word and to His holy character. Lamentations 3:22 says, "*Because of the Lord's great love we are not consumed, for His compassions never fail. They are new every morning; great is Your faithfulness. I say to myself, 'The Lord is my portion; therefore I will wait for Him.'"* Isaiah 55:11 reminds us of the faithfulness of God's Word to achieve its purposes: "... *so is my word that goes out from my mouth: It will not return to me empty, but will accomplish what I desire and achieve the purpose for which I sent it."* The cleft in the Rock is a place of trust in His faithfulness in the past (Psalm 77:10-12), and of trust in His Word to accomplish something in our lives as we continue to run to it in the time of storm. His Word can do a work within the spirit of a person without the person having a conscious awareness of its effect.

For example, when I took my last Tetanus injection, I didn't expect to feel or see anything happening in my body as my immunity level to Tetanus was raised, but when I got to the mission field where there are no modern hospitals or immune serums, I knew I could count on it to have done its work. Can we similarly trust in God's Word, faithfully input into our spirits, to have an effect deep within our spiritual man, even if our conscious minds and emotions cannot perceive it? If we can grasp this truth, we will run to feed on God's Word every chance we get within the storms of life, trusting it to have an effect on the inner man which will one day be manifest in the outer man, in God's sovereign timing and purposes.

There is an old hymn which says, *"Lead me to the Rock that is higher than I."* May God in His compassion and grace give us power to run quickly for the covering within the Rock, not wasting any precious time outside in the storm shaking our fists at Him, trying to understand all of His sometimes mysterious working in our lives through this storm.

There have been times when I have been so confused and discouraged by the circumstances I was in, that I found it almost impossible to pray. And during these times my soul or the enemy of my soul would like to suggest that there was also no hope or comfort to be found in reading God's Word. But if I will allow my spirit to speak to my soul saying, " *Why are you downcast, O my soul? Why so disturbed within me? Put your hope in God, for I will yet praise him, my Savior and my God"* (Psalm 42:5), then I will obey what I already know is the desire of my spirit man – to run to God rather than away from Him, even if I think or feel that He has disappointed me, betrayed me, wounded me or otherwise let me down. Consider Isaiah 53:4, "*Surely he took up our infirmities and carried our sorrows, yet we considered him stricken by God, smitten by Him and afflicted. But he was pierced for our transgressions, he was crushed for our iniquities; the punishment that brought us peace was upon him* ." Jesus was betrayed, wounded and let down, and yet these very blows and sufferings bought us our eternal salvation and healing in this life. Even when we feel this way, Jesus could say to us, "*Surely I have carried your sorrows",* (Isaiah 53:4). If God's grace was sufficient to sustain Jesus through His sufferings, then His grace and the Spirit of Christ in me can also sustain me through my trials.

When I became engaged to my husband, I began to share with him my daily journal from my time with God in His Word and prayer. When we were separated by a number of miles, I would mail these to him regularly. He would comment to me later that he could always tell when I was facing a tough time because I would always run into the Psalms. Once could make an interesting Bible study to read the Psalms anew and consider the number of different situations in which David found himself running to God crying for help – everything from being chased by soldiers trying to kill him, to pondering why the bad guys seemed to have it all when he was in lack, to remorse over his own terrible iniquity. Many of the trials of life have already been prayed through by David, and when we feel we can't even pray, we can let the Holy Spirit within us pray through David's and the other Psalmists' prayers for us. Try it the next time you're in a storm.

As I have written this section on storms, the Spirit of God and the notes in the margins of my worn Bible have brought to mind dozens of verses that He has used to speak to me when the storm was so loud I didn't think I could even hear Him speaking. I have prayerfully considered sharing more of these with you here. But I believe I am to leave them unmentioned, allowing you the life-changing experience of discovering them for yourself. God has promised in Isaiah 45:3, "*I will give you the treasures of darkness, riches stored in secret places, so that you may know that I am the Lord, the God of Israel, who summons you by name.*"

In looking in the margins of two well-worn Bibles over past 15 years, I see that some of my greatest treasures from God's Word were found amidst the darkness of the darkest storms.

My prayer is that we can begin to trust that even in this dark storm there is hidden a rich treasure, and one which He may give us opportunity to share with others at some later date. In retrospect we can see that sometimes when we didn't think God was present and speaking, He was actually vitally alive and at work within us, speaking truths to our spirit almost too profound for words. I have heard wise men say that "hind-sight is 20/20." And I think we will do well to remind ourselves in the midst of a storm, that there will be a future date when the events of this season will come into clearer focus, and make more sense than they do now. Lord, help us trust Your infinite love and good purposes in our lives.

But while on the subject of storms, let's take a look at one other aspect of storms which bears considering. In the Luke 8:19-25 story, Jesus told His disciples that they were going on over to the other side of the lake. A storm blew up, and the disciples feared for their lives. In Ephesians 2:2, Satan is described as the "*ruler of the kingdom of the air.*" When Jesus "*rebuked the winds*" in the Matthew 823-34 story about the storm, He actually took dominion over the powers of Satan that were trying to prevent their crossing.

Why was Satan concerned about their crossing? Because he knew that on the other side there awaited a demonic man filled with a legion of demons, and he also knew Jesus had authority over them. When this man was delivered from his demons, he spread the Word of Christ to the Decapolis, a region of 10 cities. I believe it was this very powerful spread of the message of his deliverance by Jesus Christ which the enemy tried to prevent with a nasty storm on the "way over to the other side". When we get in the middle of an untimely quarrel or upset, we need to examine where we are headed and be on our guard.

Now, especially for those of you in ministry or mission positions, take heed! The enemy will often try to stir up a storm when you are on your way to the other side of something to bring the deliverance of Jesus Christ and His Name. I could tell you story after story of how the enemy has done this when we are on our way to minister to a prayer group, a church meeting, or preparing to leave for a mission trip on the other side of the world for a sizable duration of time and a potential for significant impact.

But it just so happens that this particular truth is very real to me in the moment of writing this chapter. My husband left for the mission field nearly two weeks ago, and I am due to leave in five days to join him there for an extended period of mission projects. Within the past month we have experienced a short in our downstairs electric circuits requiring us to obtain the services of an electrician to repair it. The clutch went out on our car two weeks ago as we were participating in an extended fast for hunger and famine relief with our youth group. At the same time we had an unusual sound in our furnace, and were informed by the furnace repairman that it had become faulty and would to be replaced (a several thousand dollar project). The heater went out on our car, and we haven't had time or chosen to use resources to repair it, even though it went out in winter. Just yesterday I left for work an hour early to find a service shop to repair or purchase a new tire for the car, for a minor mishap with a curb two day before had ruined a tire. I finally was successful, and made it to the mission office in time for our weekly prayer time. Then on my way to my part-time job at our local hospital, another tire also went flat for no apparent reason. I rescheduled appointments for my work, and spent another ninety minutes getting that tire repaired also. So several hours of a day with an already bulging "to do" list had been eaten up.

I rushed home to grab a few things before running to the church to fill in for my husband in his position with our youth group's evening meeting. I reached under the kitchen sink to grab a paper bag, and accidentally tipped over a small fire extinguisher. The top popped off when it hit the kitchen floor, and the white powder was soon spewing vigorously around the room. This really challenged my resolve to learn to praise God and give Him thanks in all circumstances, as I had to stop long enough to open doors and sweep up at least the worst of the white powder storm. To make matters worse, there are documents I need to finish writing quickly in preparation for the trip, and the printer with my used computer at home as well as the one at the mission office have both decided not to work for several days. (Thankfully they are now restored). And that is not the end of the list of stormy events which have made it even harder to complete the necessary tasks for the busiest time of my year. You may have similar stories of storms like these in your life.

Having experienced this type of storm quite a number of times now, there at least two things we are learning:

First, when we are "going to the other side" to do work for the Kingdom of Jesus Christ, there will be winds and storms blown up in order to try to hinder, delay, or even stop the work. We must expect this tactic of our enemy, and be prepared for it. We must set our faces to push through to the other side, even if it means some issues will be postponed till later. The burned out furnace, the car without a clutch, the broken car heater will all be waiting for us when we return from the "other side." Then God will either provide the resources for repair, the grace to wait for resources, or the grace to give these things up.

I heard a report earlier this week from a team leader just returning from a mission effort in Vietnam. As he shared some of the sufferings of the "persecuted Church," I realized these little squalls needed to come into perspective in my thinking. Sometimes we only think we are paying a price to participate in the spread of the gospel, when the real price is being paid by those imprisoned and martyred for Jesus' sake and for His Kingdom.

Secondly, I believe God is trying to teach us all something powerful when we experience storms like this. We need to recognize the tactics of the enemy and learn to take authority over them in the Name and blood of Jesus Christ of Nazareth. We need to dress ourselves in the full armor of God (Ephesians 6:10-17), so that we can learn to stand steadfast when the fiery darts come at us from every direction. The Holy Spirit promises to lead us into truth, and as we ask Him for insight and spiritual discernment at these times, He will begin to teach us through them. Or He may use other persons or resources at our disposal to teach us some offensive and defensive strategies to counter this type of stormy season. But remember, the Holy Spirit will always be the best teacher, never contradicting the clear teaching of the Word of God.

When we find ourselves in the midst of some apparent opposition such as this as we prepare to minister to God's people in some capacity, there are some who will say, "You are having a lot of difficulty getting going at this; perhaps it's not the Lord's Will at all. Maybe you're acting in the flesh, trying to force open a door which He hasn't opened." You may well have heard some words very similar to these. These are times when we must remember back to His original order to us "to go," which hopefully was confirmed to us at that time with a testimony of two or three witnesses. Jesus brought forward an Old Testament pattern in His teaching recorded in Matthew 18:16, which says, "... *that every matter may be established by the testimony of two or three witnesses.*" If our current plans have been confirmed in such a way, we must hang onto this in faith believing, understanding that one confirming sign that we are in the center of God's Will is that there will be some kind of opposition from the enemy, especially if our potential ministry action is a threat to his kingdom. If there is no opposition at all, then we must seek God and be sure that we have heard His Word correctly. One mature Christian sister with whom I shared the recent story of my flat tires and the fire extinguisher episode, she just laughed and said, "Well, you must be right where God wants you then."

There are times when even a well-meaning brother or sister in Christ may give us what they feel is a "word" from the Lord that we are not to go forward to do this ministry, or that we should not go at this time. If this happens to you, go back and remember His original word to you and the testimony of two or more witnesses which helped to propel you in this direction. Then hang onto it, remembering that most of the opposition Jesus faced was from religious leaders of His time, and some of ours will be also.

If we read the biographical accounts of some of the world's greatest missionaries, we will see that they faced all kinds of trials and difficulties as they prepared to go as He had directed them. For a reminder of this, pick up the story of Hudson Taylor's life, "*Spiritual Secrets.*" His methods of taking inland China for Christ were straight out of God's heart, but they were often confronted by even the mission board who had originally sent him to the mission field in China.

In the past I have asked the Lord why He allows these difficult and trying things to touch our lives. After all, "I am going out on His behalf into His harvest field." I felt this is the answer God gave me on more than one occasion: He said He allows these things in order to remind me that I am going into a battle zone, reminding me that we take His Kingdom from the enemy by force. Matthew 11:12 says, "... *the Kingdom of Heaven has been forcefully advancing and forceful men lay hold of it.*" The enemy has come to "*steal, kill and destroy*" (John 10:10), and he will not sleep while we attempt or even prepare to seize a part of his kingdom away from him. We should consider Isaiah 61:1 or Jesus' quotation of it in Luke 4:18-19 regarding His understanding of His mission and the quick rejection and opposition to it by the religious leaders: "*The Spirit of the Lord is on me, because He has anointed me to preach good news to the poor; He has sent me to proclaim freedom for the prisoners and recovery of sight for the blind, to release the oppressed, to proclaim the year of the Lord's favor.*" At this declaration the people in the synagogue became furious, and they even tried to throw him down a cliff (verse 29).

I felt Holy Spirit told me that He allows some flack to come to us from the enemy in order to help us stay alert and praying, always depending on Him for both our offense and our defense. I Peter 5:7-11 reminds us to "*Cast all your anxiety on him because He cares for you. Be self-controlled and alert. Your enemy the devil prowls around like a roaring lion looking for someone to devour. Resist him, standing firm in the faith, because you know that your brothers throughout the world are undergoing the same kind of sufferings. And the God of all grace, who called you to his eternal glory in Christ, after you have suffered a little while, will himself restore you and make you strong, firm and steadfast. To Him be the power for ever and ever. Amen.*" If we had no signs that we were approaching "enemy territory," we would not get prepared to stand alert and ready for action.

I am reminded that soldiers who go to the front lines for combat are trained in advance with months and sometimes years of simulated combat experience, so they are ready to craw on their bellies to dodge bullets and to test a field for land mines. If God allowed me to experience no opposition from the enemy, I would be ignorant, naïve, and unable to stand in the face of far more severe trials and opposition in the midst of the mission field. He is our Jehovah Nissi, the captain under whom we train and draw our resources. His grace will help us learn to respond quickly to His commands, both in the training times and in the actual fierce battles.

Storms of life are common to all of us. They can cause us to stumble in our walk with God if we are not prepared for them and ready to take cover under His wings. Psalm 17:8-9 reads, "*Keep me as the apple of your eye; hide me in the shadow of your wings from the wicked who assail me, from my mortal enemies who surround me.*" This is why I have taken so long to discuss this section on storms, but I will soon go on to the O of SOON.

THE SECRET IN THE STORM

"Grace and peace to you from God our Father and the Lord Jesus Christ. Praise be to the God and Father of our Lord Jesus Christ, the Father of compassion and the God of all comfort, Who comforts us in all our troubles, so that we can comfort those in any trouble with the comfort we ourselves have received from God." *(2 Corinthians 1:2-4)*

Oh Lord, it's when I'm overwhelmed
With the trials of this life,
Your comfort seems to overflow
To help me through the strife.

For truly You are that Solid Rock
That doesn't seem to move, (Psalm 40:2)
As the storms of life overwhelm me,
With waves of pain that shove.

But even in darkest shadows
I know that You are there.
Your promises remind me
Of Your constant love and care.

But sometimes You seem distant
From my place of doubt and pain.
I need reminders of Your love
Reaching out to me again.

It's then You touch me through a friend...
When my sorrows flood like rain.
When sleepless hours taunt me
Saying, "You'll never feel good again."

Oh, its then Your Spirit comforts me
First this way, and then another,
Embracing me like strong warm hugs
Like a gentle loving mother.

Lord, why You once put "skin on"
Is a mystery to me.
How You left Your throne of glory
With all its majesty. (Philippians 2:6-7)

You walked the earth like we do
Through the sorrows and the pains.
You suffered, bled and died to carry
Each of these for our gain. (Isaiah 53:4-5)

But by the Father's touch You rose
From the darkest painful pit,
To take Your place upon Your throne
For eternity to sit. (Ephesians 1:19-23)

And from there You send Your Spirit
To those who heed Your Word
And follow in the footsteps
Of their Savior and their Lord. (Acts 2:33)

Now You come again with "skin on" (Phil. 2:7)
To our world of trials and pains.
And through those who bear Your Spirit
You reach out to us again. (Phil. 2:1-2)

You reach out in ways that we can feel
In our silent lonely place,
With touches that are tangible
We can receive Your grace. (2 Cor. 1:3-7)

Through one you'll bring a silent smile
That says, "I understand."
Through another there's a gentle touch
From a silent outstretched hand.

Then finally my eyes awake
To see the waves grow still.
And the beacon of the lighthouse
So strong on nearby hill.

You bid me come and climb with You
        To that place of higher ground.
You point out this one...and then that one,
        As we strain to look around.

You say, "*You see them don't you?*"
        As they founder in the sea.
"The storm is overwhelming them;
        They need a touch from Me."

"Will you take this line I've given you
        And throw it out to them?
While their waves of loneliness and pain
        Don't seem to have an end?

"I can not leave My watch here...
        But will you go for me?
And give to them what I gave you
        As you tossed upon the sea?"

"You are My hands...you are My feet
        Now go, prepared to share. (*Isa. 50:4-5*)
Can't you see they're waiting desperately
        To feel My tender care?"

Then I say, "But what could I do
        To ease their bed of pain?
How could I ever bring the Light
        To comfort them again?"

You say, "*But it's so simple*!"
        Your soft eyes pierce me through.
"You only have to give to them
        What I have given you." (Jn. 14:27)

With that same love and comfort
        You can reach out to them,
As the waves are crashing violently
        They can know Hope again. (Rom. 15:13)

...So now, don't tarry longer
In this safe and peaceful place.
Run now and go to comfort them
With My love and with My grace.(Jn. 1-9)

With your voice you can whisper
My enduring love and care.
When your hands reach out to them
They'll know that I am there.

With the comfort that I gave to you
Now go to those you see. (2 Cor. 1:4)
And you'll find the sweetness of my love
Is poured out sufficiently.

For My love is never ending,
Unyielding as the grave.
My love is even stronger
Than any crashing wave. (SOS 8:6-7)

It burns like blazing fire,
And like a mighty flame.
No water can e'er quench it
Unchanging as my Name. (SOS 8:6-7)

No worldly wealth can buy it
A pearl of endless worth. (Matt. 13:45-46)
So freely give My love away,
And find it still is yours to stay.

Janice. Woodrum

Chapter Thirteen

Obstinate

The first O of the word "soon" is for OBSTINATE. I can almost see the hair bristle on your neck as you read the word. "Not me," you say... "I am seeking the presence and the word of the Lord." I went to Webster's dictionary for some insight into the word obstinate, and a definition is "strongly adhering to an opinion, purpose, or course in spite of reason, arguments or persuasion (a perverse or unreasonable persistence)." A synonym is "stubborn", which implies sturdiness in resisting attempts to change or abandon a course or opinion. Another is "Mulish", which implies a thoroughly unreasonable obstinacy, and yet another is "Dogged" which suggests a tenacious, frequently sullen persistence. These word images don't paint a very pretty picture, and most of us will immediately think that this could never be a reason for a drought or dark period in our lives.

But let us each examine ourselves again. What does this have to do with me? Has there ever been a time when I listened for God to tell me what I wanted to hear? And He didn't. So I asked again and listened and even fasted and listened some more, and He still didn't tell me what I wanted to hear. So I concluded that I just wasn't hearing from God, and sank into a depressed period because of it.

This reminds me of a young child who asks for something from his mother such as an ice cream bar just before dinnertime. She says, "No, we must wait until after dinner." But he persists and keeps asking again and again, only to get the same answer. It is easy for us to see that a good parent will hold to what he/she has said, and will not bring out an ice cream until after the meal. We would think that a weak or poor parent might get tired of the whining and go ahead and give the child an ice cream bar to keep him quiet. Hebrews 12 says that God our Father disciplines the sons He loves. He is not likely to spoil us by giving us what we are demanding in our obstinate, unyielding point of view. If He does give in, we will only throw a bigger tantrum next time to get our own way. Galatians 6:7 says, "*Do not be deceived; God cannot be mocked*..." God won't play this kind of game with us; He may simply ignore us until we get over our tantrum. Thus we enter into a period of drought, not experiencing a fresh word or sense of His presence for awhile.

I see two issues at play here if we are to overcome this childish pattern. The first is an absolute conviction upon the sovereignty of God. He maintains all rights to do what He wants to do the way He wants to do it and when He wants to do it. "*You are the potter; I am the clay. Mold me and make me; this is what I pray.*" It may be easy to sing, but much harder to live out in our lives when our own preferences and desires are at stake. I am a firm believer that sometimes "we have not because we ask not". But when He says "*No" or "Wait*", or no clear answer at all for a season, can we abandon ourselves to His sovereignty in His choice of when He will answer, His choice of if or when He will explain what He has been doing, or what His answer will be? If we are unable or unwilling to do this, the result will sometimes be that we become angry with God. David Henderson wrote in an article about humility that stated, "Anger can mean I am not trusting God's sovereign plan and timing, and am trying to take control from Him." We need to ask ourselves truthfully, "Is our problem that God isn't speaking to us, or is it that He isn't saying what we want to hear?" We need to let the Holy Spirit search our hearts for an obstinate or stubborn root, which is nothing more than the old self wanting its own way. He can exchange our heart of stone for a heart of flesh ... a heart that is yielded to what God has chosen for us. *"I will give them an undivided heart and put a new spirit in them; I will remove from them their heart of stone and give them a heart of flesh"* (Ezekiel 11:19).

The second issue at play here is servanthood. Sometimes we make excuses for not serving as ministers to others because we have not had the ____________________ which we thought we needed to do the job. You can insert whatever fits into the blank space. It might be talent, fluent speech, opportunity for education, good health, finances, giftings, experience, family support, intelligence, and the list could go on and on.

Sometimes we don't think we are hearing from God, because we are expecting some loftier instructions or assignment or lot in life than we are getting. Or else we aren't able to trust Him to empower us if the task we are hearing Him assign seems beyond our own reach. We may pass this hearing off as just our own imagination. But if we are willing to let the Holy Spirit align our minds to that of Christ Jesus, who "*made himself nothing, taking the very nature of a servant*" (Philippians 2:7), then He will give us a contentment in whatever avenue of service He might direct us to at any particular stage of our life.

I spoke recently with a precious sister who just returned form a mission experience in India. She has a voice like a lark, and is gifted with strong abilities in preaching and teaching. But on this trip God used her primarily in the area of prayer and prophecy into individual lives of people who were waiting and hungry for a touch from God. She had few opportunities to serve as she expected to serve. I asked her if this had been painful for her, requiring a death to what the self wanted. But she responded that God's grace had abounded in contentment, being used according to His wishes, and allowing God to round out her ministry by instruction and experience in areas where she had been weak before.

Richard Foster gives a slightly different definition to the role of choosing to serve or choosing to be a servant, in his work *Celebration of Discipline*. He says, "choosing to serve allows me to stay comfortably in charge. I decide when, where, and whom I will serve. This kind of service can actually produce pride rather than humility, as the focus remains on what is good for me. On the other hand, when I choose to be a servant, I have placed myself 'on call' to the needs of others" (Haughty or Humble by Howard Baker, Discipleship

Journal May-June, 1998). Part of being able to hear the voice of God is a heart that is *willing* to hear what He has to say.

Will I yield to His choice, or in an ever so subtle obstinate attitude want to maintain the control over whom I serve and when? These are difficult questions to ask ourselves, and the living out of this kind of abandonment is even more difficult. But I think Paul had found some of it when he wrote, *"I have learned to be content whatever the circumstances."* Sovereign Lord help us begin to want to be abandoned to all your choices for us. Amen.

Chapter Fourteen

Overconfidence

The word OVERCONFIDENCE reminds me of dealing with an adolescent child. He needs to learn to do some things for himself that he had previously not done before, because his mom or dad had done them all his life. So when he thinks he can do it himself, mom and dad suddenly aren't nearly as smart as he thought they were all his thirteen years. Sometimes we as parents just need to take hands off, letting our adolescents try for themselves and often experience that they weren't quite as smart or adept as they thought they were. Then when they are a little older, they may actually come and ask us to share with them some of the wisdom we have gained through the years of experience or study.

Jesus said that if we are to enter the Kingdom of God, we must become like little children. Herein lies a paradox. He wants us to mature in our Christian faith *"... until we all reach unity in the faith and in the knowledge of the Son of God and become mature, attaining to the whole measure of the fullness of Christ"* (Ephesians 4:13), but He always wants us to maintain a childlike dependence upon Him. As a matter of fact, the more we learn to depend on Him and the less we rely on ourselves, the more we will find ourselves walking in the Spirit rather than the flesh. Good old Proverbs 3:6-7 says, *"in all your ways acknowledge him, and he will make your paths straight. Do not be wise in your own eyes; fear the Lord and shun evil."* Hosea 6:3 says, *"Let us acknowledge the Lord; let us press on to acknowledge Him."* This is really the cry of my heart – that I would be able to turn to Him in every thought, word and deed which I undertake throughout every day, and acknowledge His choice, His wisdom, His judgment, and His understanding rather than my own. I believe herein lies much of the secret of the command to "*pray without ceasing*" and a practical application of walking in the Spirit. How could a loving Daddy keep quiet when His sweet daughter keeps saying, "What do you think about this Daddy? Will you help me do this; I'm not big enough?" Or, "Please tell me how to tie my shoe." Jesus, our ultimate role model said, in John 12:49, "*For I did not speak of my own accord, but the Father who sent me commanded me what to say and how to say it. I know that His command leads to eternal life. So whatever I say is just what the Father has told me to say.*" This kind of confidence in God, rather than in myself is a predominant goal of my life.

Another reminder of this same principle is found in Philippians 4:12b-13, "*I have learned the secret of being content in any and every situation, whether well fed or hungry, whether living in plenty or in want. I can do everything through Him who gives me strength.*" His contentment, not mine; His strength, not mine. And in 2 Corinthians 12:9-10 he says, "*But He said to me, 'My grace is sufficient for you, for my power is made perfect in weakness. Therefore I will boast all the more gladly about my weaknesses, so that Christ's power may rest on me ... For when I am weak, then I am strong.' "* But he really sums it up in 2 Corinthians 3:4-6, *"Such confidence as this is ours through Christ before God. Not that we are competent in ourselves to claim anything for ourselves, but our competence comes from God. He has made us competent as ministers of a new covenant – not of the letter but of the Spirit; for the letter kills, but the Spirit gives life."*

I think every one of us could hear more from God than we do if we would throw aside more of our "I can do it myself" attitude, and take on the attitude of Christ who said, "*whatever I say is just what the Father has told me to say.*" Wow, that's pretty much constant hearing, and His Spirit works in us to make it more of a reality in our lives every day as we yield ourselves to Him.

Chapter Fifteen

Need

The end of the word "soon," and the end of this book is the N which stands for NEED. Do we always seek the presence of God to meet our own need, or do we come into His presence in order to please Him? This question is a real eye opener for me, for if I am honest with myself, even my worship of Him is often motivated by the desire to experience an awareness of His presence and bask in its warmth. Or I may worship to see Him in His great majesty, power and sovereignty so that I may have more faith to believe that He can really handle this situation which is beyond my own strength, wisdom or endurance. And too often the only reason I seek His presence is because I need something from Him. We just examined in the last "O" that this kind of dependence is within His will for us, but when it's all we come to Him for, we fall immeasurably short of the sweet fellowship which I believe God wants us to experience with Him. Wouldn't the Daddy in my above example be disappointed if his daughter came to him only wanting His help? Wouldn't there be times when the pleasure of the Daddy would be to just hold her on His lap? Oh my, we just mentioned a brand new idea – His pleasure, not mine.

How often do we desire to hear from God or experience a sense of His presence because we sense a need for it in our own life, and how often do we want to come into His presence *just to bring pleasure to His heart?* Perhaps you are familiar with the writing of Jeanne Guyon, who several hundred years ago wrote some of the most profound thoughts about experiencing God in our lives. I want to quote a passage from her book, "*Experiencing the Depths of Jesus Christ.*"

" I would like to talk with you just a moment about the motive of your heart in your seeking the Lord. After all, why

do you come to the Lord? Do you come to Him for the sweetness? Do you come to Him because it is enjoyable to be in the Lord's presence? Let me recommend a higher way.

As you come to the Lord to pray, bring a full heart of pure love, a love that is not seeking anything itself. Bring a heart that is seeking nothing from the Lord, but desires only to please Him and do His will.

Let me illustrate. Consider the servant. The servant takes good care of His master; but if he does it only to receive some reward, he is not worthy of any consideration whatsoever. So, dear Christian, as you come to your Lord to pray, do not come for spiritual enjoyment. Do not even come to experience your Lord.

Then what? Come just to please Him.

Once you are there, if He chooses to pour out some great blessing, receive it. But if, instead, if your mind wanders, receive that. Or if you have a difficult time in prayer, receive that. Joyfully accept whatever He desires to give. Believer that whatever happens is what He wants to give you!

Let me repeat that, for it is very important! It is especially important to you for any future growth in experiencing Christ. Believe by faith that whatever happens is His desire for you at that time.

When you have come to the Lord this way, you will find that your spirit is at peace no matter what your condition. When you have learned to come to the Lord with this attitude, you will not be upset if the Lord withdraws Himself from you. The times of spiritual dryness will be the same to you as the times of spiritual abundance. You will treat them both the same. Why? Because you will have learned to love God just because you love Him, not because of His gifts, nor even for His precious presence."

And with that I will leave you exactly where I find myself at this moment – trying to digest these profound statements about a degree of love which I rarely have experienced.

And also with one verse that encourages me in this quest: I Corinthians 13:12, "*Now we see but a poor reflection as in a mirror; then we shall see face to face. Now I know in part; then*

I shall know fully, even as I am fully known." Oswald Chambers is a world famous hero in the realm of daily devotions with God, for his beloved wife compiled some of His writings into the devotional, "*My Utmost for His Highest.*" Oswald died at an early age of a serious infection. During the days in the hospital when he was critically ill, his wife felt she had heard a word from the Lord that this illness would not be unto death. But God wasn't promising a relief from physical death, but a promise of eternal life, for within a few days he did pass from this life. She must have been left with a little wondering about what she had heard from God. But her questioning didn't changer her indisputable faith in the God they had served so faithfully together. As she prepared to send a telegram to family members informing them of his death, she chose these few words: "OSWALD, IN HIS PRESENCE." All of his family immediately understood the meaning of her brief wire. And we who have embraced the salvation which comes through Jesus Christ alone and His Lordship of our lives have this assurance: there will come a day for each of us when we know and see clearly that which is now only a poor reflection. "... then we shall see face to face."

Hallelujah!

A little song was composed* to help remember the different titles of the chapters of this book, in order to make a periodic evaluation of "How am I doing?" without needing to refer back to the book. Perhaps you'll want to make up your own melody to this fun little self-test, and see how you score from month to month, year to year, and decade to decade – until you see Him face to face and we become like Him, beholding Him as he really is.

* *Hope To Hear Soon song* by Amber Woodrum

H	Have I been ***honest*** with you, Lord, bringing the truth of my heart to you?
O	Am I ***obedient*** to what you tell me to do?
P	Am I ***persuaded*** you're always near?
E	Always ***expecting*** to hear?
T	***Trusting*** in your faithfulness, too?
O	Do I ***offer*** all I can, thanking you again and again?
H	Do I ***hunger*** for your presence and thirst for your Word?
E	Do I have ***empathy*** for others? Do I ***enjoy*** the Spirit you in them? Am I ***encouraging*** whenever I can?
A	Could I ***abandon*** myself more fully? Or am I surrendered to you?
R	Do I ***rest*** in your Sovereignty, too?
S	Would I seek You in the midst of a ***storm***?
O	Or am I ***obstinate*** and so stubborn?
O	Am I ***overconfident*** to a fault?
N	***Needing*** you, because I don't want to be without?

HOPE TO HEAR SOON, I HOPE TO HEAR SOON...
I WILL ALWAYS LOOK TO HEAR WHAT I CAN HEAR FROM YOU!

CPSIA information can be obtained at www.ICGtesting.com
Printed in the USA
BVOW080005070613

322666BV00001B/42/P